# 50 International Snacks and Appetizers

By: Kelly Johnson

# Table of Contents

- Empanadas (Argentina)
- Sushi Rolls (Japan)
- Samosas (India)
- Spring Rolls (Vietnam)
- Guacamole with Tortilla Chips (Mexico)
- Tapenade (France)
- Arancini (Italy)
- Hummus with Pita (Middle East)
- Falafel (Middle East)
- Banh Mi (Vietnam)
- Ceviche (Peru)
- Baklava (Turkey)
- Churros (Spain)
- Queso Fundido (Mexico)
- Poffertjes (Netherlands)
- Gyoza (Japan)
- Kimchi (Korea)
- Empanadillas (Spain)
- Poutine (Canada)
- Tzatziki with Pita (Greece)
- Mini Quiches (France)
- Anticuchos (Peru)
- Mezze Platter (Middle East)
- Cheese Fondue (Switzerland)
- Fritters (Jamaica)
- Dolmas (Greece)
- Kue Cubir (Indonesia)
- Cornbread (USA)
- Chana Chaat (India)
- Tacos (Mexico)
- Pão de Queijo (Brazil)
- Blini with Caviar (Russia)
- Dim Sum (China)
- Croquettes (France)
- Bruschetta (Italy)

- Cucumber Sandwiches (England)
- Tostones (Puerto Rico)
- Shakshuka (Israel)
- Sautéed Edamame (Japan)
- Prawn Toast (China)
- Pastelitos (Cuba)
- Borscht with Sour Cream (Ukraine)
- Arepas (Colombia)
- Roti Canai (Malaysia)
- Meat Pie (Australia)
- Sarmale (Romania)
- Keftedes (Greece)
- Patatas Bravas (Spain)
- Vareniki (Ukraine)
- Malasadas (Portugal)

## Empanadas (Argentina)

### Ingredients:

- 1 package empanada dough (store-bought or homemade)
- 1 lb ground beef or chicken
- 1 small onion, chopped
- 1/2 red bell pepper, chopped
- 1/4 cup olives, chopped (green or black)
- 1/4 cup raisins (optional)
- 1/2 teaspoon cumin
- 1/2 teaspoon paprika
- Salt and pepper to taste
- 1 egg (for egg wash)

### Instructions:

1. Preheat the oven to 375°F (190°C). Heat a skillet over medium heat and sauté the onions and bell pepper until softened, about 5 minutes.
2. Add the ground beef or chicken to the skillet and cook until browned. Season with cumin, paprika, salt, and pepper. Stir in the olives and raisins, if using. Remove from heat and allow to cool.
3. Roll out the empanada dough on a floured surface and cut into circles (about 5-6 inches in diameter). Spoon the filling onto the center of each circle.
4. Fold the dough over to create a half-moon shape and crimp the edges to seal.
5. Brush the empanadas with beaten egg and bake for 20-25 minutes, or until golden brown. Serve warm.

## Sushi Rolls (Japan)

**Ingredients:**

- 2 cups sushi rice, cooked and cooled
- 4 sheets nori (seaweed)
- 1/2 lb sushi-grade fish (tuna, salmon, etc.), thinly sliced
- 1 cucumber, julienned
- 1 avocado, sliced
- 2 tablespoons rice vinegar
- 1 tablespoon sugar
- Soy sauce for dipping
- Pickled ginger (optional)
- Wasabi (optional)

**Instructions:**

1. In a small bowl, combine rice vinegar and sugar. Stir until the sugar dissolves, then mix it into the cooled sushi rice.
2. Place a sheet of nori on a bamboo sushi mat, shiny side down. Spread a thin layer of rice over the nori, leaving a small border at the top.
3. Arrange fish, cucumber, and avocado along the center of the rice.
4. Roll the sushi tightly using the mat, sealing the edge with a little water.
5. Slice the roll into bite-sized pieces. Serve with soy sauce, pickled ginger, and wasabi.

## Samosas (India)

### Ingredients:

- 2 large potatoes, boiled and mashed
- 1/2 cup peas, cooked
- 1 small onion, chopped
- 2 cloves garlic, minced
- 1 tablespoon ginger, minced
- 1 teaspoon cumin seeds
- 1 teaspoon coriander powder
- 1 teaspoon garam masala
- 1/2 teaspoon turmeric powder
- 1/2 teaspoon chili powder (optional)
- Salt to taste
- 1 package samosa pastry sheets (store-bought or homemade)
- Oil for frying

### Instructions:

1. Heat a little oil in a pan and sauté cumin seeds, onion, garlic, and ginger until fragrant.
2. Add the mashed potatoes, peas, coriander, garam masala, turmeric, chili powder, and salt. Stir well to combine, then remove from heat and let cool.
3. Cut the samosa pastry into strips and form into cone shapes. Fill each cone with the potato mixture and seal the edges.
4. Heat oil in a deep pan and fry the samosas until golden and crispy, about 4-5 minutes. Drain on paper towels and serve with tamarind chutney or mint chutney.

## Spring Rolls (Vietnam)

**Ingredients:**

- 1 cup cooked shrimp, chopped
- 1/2 cup vermicelli noodles, cooked
- 1/2 cucumber, julienned
- 1/4 cup fresh mint leaves
- 1/4 cup fresh cilantro leaves
- 1/4 cup fresh basil leaves
- 8 rice paper wrappers
- 1/4 cup hoisin sauce
- 1 tablespoon peanut butter (optional)

**Instructions:**

1. Prepare all ingredients by chopping and prepping them as described.
2. Fill a shallow bowl with warm water. Submerge a rice paper wrapper in the water for 10-15 seconds to soften.
3. Lay the softened wrapper on a clean surface and place a small portion of shrimp, noodles, cucumber, and herbs in the center.
4. Fold the sides in and roll up tightly to seal.
5. Serve the spring rolls with hoisin peanut dipping sauce made by mixing hoisin sauce and peanut butter.

**Guacamole with Tortilla Chips (Mexico)**

**Ingredients:**

- 3 ripe avocados, peeled and mashed
- 1 small onion, finely chopped
- 1 tomato, diced
- 1 jalapeño, finely chopped (optional)
- 1 tablespoon lime juice
- Salt and pepper to taste
- Tortilla chips for serving

**Instructions:**

1. In a bowl, mash the avocados until smooth with some texture.
2. Add onion, tomato, jalapeño, lime juice, salt, and pepper. Stir gently to combine.
3. Serve immediately with tortilla chips for dipping.

## Tapenade (France)

### Ingredients:

- 1 cup Kalamata olives, pitted
- 1/2 cup green olives, pitted
- 2 tablespoons capers
- 1/4 cup olive oil
- 1 tablespoon fresh lemon juice
- 1 teaspoon fresh thyme (optional)
- 1 clove garlic, minced

### Instructions:

1. Combine the olives, capers, olive oil, lemon juice, thyme, and garlic in a food processor.
2. Pulse until the mixture reaches a chunky paste consistency.
3. Serve the tapenade with crusty bread or crackers.

## Arancini (Italy)

**Ingredients:**

- 2 cups cooked risotto (preferably leftover)
- 1/2 cup mozzarella cheese, cubed
- 1/4 cup grated Parmesan cheese
- 1 egg, beaten
- 1 cup breadcrumbs
- Oil for frying
- Marinara sauce for dipping

**Instructions:**

1. Shape the cooled risotto into small balls, placing a cube of mozzarella in the center of each.
2. Dip the balls into the beaten egg, then coat with breadcrumbs.
3. Heat oil in a deep pan and fry the arancini until golden brown, about 3-4 minutes.
4. Serve with marinara sauce.

**Hummus with Pita (Middle East)**

**Ingredients:**

- 1 can (15 oz) chickpeas, drained and rinsed
- 1/4 cup tahini
- 2 tablespoons olive oil
- 1 garlic clove
- 1 tablespoon lemon juice
- 1 teaspoon cumin
- Salt to taste
- Fresh pita bread for serving

**Instructions:**

1. In a food processor, combine chickpeas, tahini, olive oil, garlic, lemon juice, cumin, and salt.
2. Process until smooth, adding more olive oil or water if needed to reach desired consistency.
3. Serve the hummus with fresh pita bread.

## Falafel (Middle East)

**Ingredients:**

- 1 cup dried chickpeas, soaked overnight
- 1/2 onion, chopped
- 2 cloves garlic, minced
- 1/4 cup fresh parsley
- 1/4 cup fresh cilantro
- 1 teaspoon cumin
- 1 teaspoon coriander
- Salt and pepper to taste
- 1 teaspoon baking powder
- 4-6 tablespoons flour
- Oil for frying

**Instructions:**

1. Drain and rinse the chickpeas. In a food processor, combine chickpeas, onion, garlic, parsley, cilantro, cumin, coriander, salt, and pepper. Pulse until mixture is coarse but sticks together.
2. Add baking powder and flour, and pulse until combined. Chill the mixture for at least 1 hour.
3. Shape the mixture into small balls or patties and fry in hot oil for 3-4 minutes until golden brown.
4. Serve with pita bread, tahini sauce, or salad.

## Banh Mi (Vietnam)

**Ingredients:**

- 1 baguette or French bread roll
- 1/2 lb cooked pork (or tofu for a vegetarian version)
- 1/4 cup mayonnaise
- 1 tablespoon sriracha (optional)
- Pickled carrots and daikon radish (or fresh if preferred)
- Fresh cilantro
- Sliced cucumber
- Jalapeño slices (optional)

**Instructions:**

1. Slice the baguette lengthwise, leaving one side attached. Spread mayonnaise on the inside of the bread.
2. Layer in the cooked pork, pickled vegetables, cilantro, cucumber, and jalapeños.
3. Serve immediately, or wrap to enjoy later.

## Ceviche (Peru)

**Ingredients:**

- 1 lb fresh firm white fish (such as tilapia or snapper), cubed
- 1/2 red onion, thinly sliced
- 1-2 jalapeños, finely chopped (optional)
- 1/2 cup fresh lime juice (about 4-5 limes)
- 1/4 cup fresh cilantro, chopped
- 1 ripe avocado, diced
- Salt and pepper to taste

**Instructions:**

1. In a glass or non-reactive bowl, combine the fish cubes, red onion, and jalapeños.
2. Pour lime juice over the mixture, ensuring the fish is fully covered. Stir gently, then cover and refrigerate for 2-3 hours, or until the fish appears "cooked" (opaque).
3. Once the fish is ready, stir in the cilantro and avocado. Season with salt and pepper to taste.
4. Serve chilled, ideally with tortilla chips or toasted bread.

## Baklava (Turkey)

**Ingredients:**

- 1 package phyllo dough (about 20 sheets)
- 2 cups mixed nuts (walnuts, pistachios, or almonds), chopped
- 1 teaspoon ground cinnamon
- 1 cup unsalted butter, melted
- 1 cup sugar
- 1/2 cup water
- 1/4 cup honey
- 1 teaspoon lemon juice
- 1/2 teaspoon vanilla extract

**Instructions:**

1. Preheat the oven to 350°F (175°C). Brush a 9x13-inch baking dish with melted butter.
2. Layer 8 sheets of phyllo dough, brushing each sheet with butter. Then, sprinkle a thin layer of chopped nuts and cinnamon.
3. Repeat the layering process with 8 more sheets of phyllo dough and more nuts. Finish by layering the remaining phyllo sheets, about 8 more.
4. Cut the baklava into diamond or square shapes before baking.
5. Bake for 40-45 minutes, or until golden and crisp.
6. In a saucepan, combine sugar, water, honey, lemon juice, and vanilla. Bring to a boil, then reduce heat and simmer for about 10 minutes.
7. Pour the hot syrup over the baked baklava. Let cool completely before serving.

## Churros (Spain)

**Ingredients:**

- 1 cup water
- 2 tablespoons butter
- 1/4 teaspoon salt
- 1 cup all-purpose flour
- 2 large eggs
- 1/4 teaspoon vanilla extract
- 1/2 cup sugar
- 1 teaspoon ground cinnamon
- Oil for frying

**Instructions:**

1. In a saucepan, bring water, butter, and salt to a boil. Stir in the flour until smooth, then remove from heat.
2. Beat in the eggs one at a time, mixing until fully combined, then add the vanilla extract.
3. Heat oil in a deep pan to 375°F (190°C).
4. Transfer the dough to a piping bag with a star tip. Pipe 4-6 inch strips of dough into the hot oil, frying until golden brown and crispy, about 3-4 minutes.
5. In a small bowl, mix sugar and cinnamon. Roll the churros in the mixture while still warm.
6. Serve with a side of chocolate sauce for dipping.

## Queso Fundido (Mexico)

**Ingredients:**

- 2 cups shredded Oaxaca cheese or mozzarella
- 1/2 cup chorizo, crumbled (optional)
- 1/2 cup roasted poblano peppers, diced
- 1 small onion, finely chopped
- 1 tablespoon olive oil
- Tortilla chips or warm tortillas for serving

**Instructions:**

1. In a skillet, heat the olive oil over medium heat. Cook the chorizo until browned and cooked through. Remove from the pan and set aside.
2. In the same pan, sauté the onions and roasted poblano peppers until softened.
3. Add the cheese to the skillet, stirring until melted and creamy.
4. Stir in the cooked chorizo. Serve immediately with tortilla chips or tortillas for dipping.

## Poffertjes (Netherlands)

**Ingredients:**

- 1 1/2 cups all-purpose flour
- 1 tablespoon sugar
- 1 teaspoon active dry yeast
- 1/4 teaspoon salt
- 1 1/4 cups warm milk
- 2 eggs
- 2 tablespoons melted butter
- Powdered sugar, for serving
- Butter, for greasing the pan

**Instructions:**

1. In a bowl, whisk together flour, sugar, yeast, and salt. Add the warm milk, eggs, and melted butter. Mix until smooth.
2. Cover the batter and let it rise for about 1 hour, until doubled in size.
3. Heat a poffertjes pan (or small griddle) over medium heat and grease with butter.
4. Spoon small amounts of batter into the wells of the pan, cooking each side for 1-2 minutes until golden brown.
5. Serve hot, dusted with powdered sugar and butter.

## Gyoza (Japan)

**Ingredients:**

- 1/2 lb ground pork
- 1 cup cabbage, finely chopped
- 1/4 cup green onions, chopped
- 2 cloves garlic, minced
- 1 tablespoon ginger, minced
- 1 tablespoon soy sauce
- 1 teaspoon sesame oil
- 1 pack gyoza wrappers
- Oil for frying
- Soy sauce and rice vinegar for dipping

**Instructions:**

1. In a bowl, combine pork, cabbage, green onions, garlic, ginger, soy sauce, and sesame oil. Mix well.
2. Place a small spoonful of the mixture onto each gyoza wrapper. Wet the edges with water, fold the wrapper in half, and pinch to seal.
3. Heat oil in a skillet over medium-high heat. Fry the gyoza for 2-3 minutes, until the bottoms are golden.
4. Add a little water to the pan and cover to steam the gyoza for 4-5 minutes until fully cooked.
5. Serve with soy sauce and rice vinegar dipping sauce.

**Kimchi (Korea)**

**Ingredients:**

- 1 medium napa cabbage, chopped
- 1/4 cup sea salt
- 3 cups water
- 1 tablespoon grated ginger
- 4 cloves garlic, minced
- 1 tablespoon fish sauce
- 1 tablespoon sugar
- 2 tablespoons gochugaru (Korean chili flakes)
- 2 green onions, chopped

**Instructions:**

1. Toss the cabbage with sea salt and let it sit for 1-2 hours to wilt, then rinse with water and drain.
2. In a bowl, combine ginger, garlic, fish sauce, sugar, gochugaru, and green onions. Stir well.
3. Massage the spice mixture into the cabbage, ensuring it's fully coated.
4. Pack the mixture into a jar, pressing it down to release air bubbles. Leave at least an inch of space at the top.
5. Let the kimchi ferment at room temperature for 2-3 days, then refrigerate for up to 2 weeks.

## Empanadillas (Spain)

### Ingredients:

- 1 package empanada dough
- 1/2 lb ground beef
- 1 small onion, chopped
- 1/2 cup green olives, chopped
- 1/2 teaspoon cumin
- 1/4 teaspoon paprika
- 1 egg (for egg wash)
- Olive oil for frying

### Instructions:

1. In a pan, cook ground beef with onions, cumin, paprika, and olives. Let cool.
2. Roll out empanada dough, and place a spoonful of filling in the center.
3. Fold the dough to form a half-moon shape, sealing the edges with a fork.
4. Brush with egg wash and fry in hot oil until golden brown, about 4-5 minutes.

**Poutine (Canada)**

**Ingredients:**

- 4 large russet potatoes, peeled and cut into fries
- 2 cups beef gravy (store-bought or homemade)
- 2 cups cheese curds (preferably white cheddar)
- Oil for frying

**Instructions:**

1. Heat oil in a deep fryer or large pot to 375°F (190°C). Fry the potato fries in batches until golden and crispy, about 4-5 minutes per batch.
2. In a saucepan, heat the beef gravy until warm.
3. Place the hot fries on a plate, top with cheese curds, and pour the warm gravy over the top.
4. Serve immediately, ensuring the cheese curds melt slightly.

**Tzatziki with Pita (Greece)**

**Ingredients:**

- 1 cup Greek yogurt
- 1/2 cucumber, finely grated
- 1 tablespoon olive oil
- 1 clove garlic, minced
- 1 tablespoon fresh dill, chopped
- 1 tablespoon fresh lemon juice
- Salt and pepper to taste
- Pita bread for serving

**Instructions:**

1. In a bowl, combine Greek yogurt, cucumber, olive oil, garlic, dill, and lemon juice.
2. Stir well and season with salt and pepper to taste.
3. Serve chilled with warm pita bread for dipping.

**Mini Quiches (France)**

**Ingredients:**

- 1 sheet puff pastry or pie dough
- 3 large eggs
- 1/2 cup heavy cream
- 1/2 cup milk
- 1/2 cup grated cheese (Gruyère or cheddar)
- 1/4 cup cooked ham, chopped (optional)
- 1/4 cup sautéed spinach or mushrooms (optional)
- Salt and pepper to taste
- Fresh herbs (parsley or thyme) for garnish

**Instructions:**

1. Preheat the oven to 375°F (190°C). Grease a muffin tin or line with paper liners.
2. Roll out the puff pastry or pie dough and cut out circles to fit into the muffin tin. Press gently to line each cup.
3. In a bowl, whisk together the eggs, heavy cream, milk, salt, and pepper.
4. Divide the cheese, ham, and sautéed vegetables evenly among the muffin cups.
5. Pour the egg mixture over the fillings and bake for 15-20 minutes, until the quiches are set and golden on top.
6. Let them cool slightly before removing from the tin. Garnish with fresh herbs and serve warm or at room temperature.

## Anticuchos (Peru)

### Ingredients:

- 1 lb beef heart or sirloin, cut into 1-inch cubes
- 1/2 cup red wine vinegar
- 3 tablespoons aji panca paste (or substitute with paprika and chili powder)
- 2 cloves garlic, minced
- 1 tablespoon cumin
- 1 tablespoon soy sauce
- 2 tablespoons olive oil
- Salt and pepper to taste
- Skewers (wooden or metal)

### Instructions:

1. In a bowl, combine red wine vinegar, aji panca paste, garlic, cumin, soy sauce, olive oil, salt, and pepper. Whisk well to combine.
2. Add the beef cubes to the marinade, ensuring they are well coated. Cover and refrigerate for at least 2 hours or overnight.
3. Preheat a grill or grill pan over medium heat. Thread the marinated beef onto skewers.
4. Grill the anticuchos for 3-4 minutes on each side, until the beef is cooked to your desired level of doneness.
5. Serve with boiled potatoes and a side of spicy sauce (aji verde) if desired.

## Mezze Platter (Middle East)

**Ingredients:**

- Hummus (store-bought or homemade)
- Baba ghanoush (store-bought or homemade)
- Tzatziki (store-bought or homemade)
- Falafel (store-bought or homemade)
- Pita bread, cut into wedges
- Olives (green and black)
- Cherry tomatoes
- Cucumber, sliced
- Pickled vegetables (optional)
- Fresh herbs (parsley, mint)

**Instructions:**

1. Arrange the hummus, baba ghanoush, and tzatziki in small bowls on a large platter.
2. Place the falafel on the platter, and add pita bread wedges for dipping.
3. Add olives, cherry tomatoes, cucumber slices, and pickled vegetables to the platter.
4. Garnish with fresh herbs like parsley or mint for a vibrant touch.
5. Serve as an appetizer or light meal, allowing guests to dip and enjoy the variety of flavors.

## Cheese Fondue (Switzerland)

**Ingredients:**

- 200g Gruyère cheese, grated
- 200g Emmental cheese, grated
- 1 clove garlic, halved
- 1 cup dry white wine
- 1 tablespoon lemon juice
- 1 tablespoon cornstarch
- 2 tablespoons kirsch (cherry brandy, optional)
- Freshly ground black pepper to taste
- Freshly grated nutmeg to taste
- Crusty bread cubes for dipping

**Instructions:**

1. Rub the inside of a fondue pot with the garlic halves.
2. In a separate saucepan, heat the wine and lemon juice over medium heat, but do not let it boil.
3. Gradually add the grated cheeses to the wine, stirring constantly until the cheese melts and becomes smooth.
4. Dissolve the cornstarch in the kirsch and stir it into the cheese mixture to thicken.
5. Season with black pepper and freshly grated nutmeg.
6. Transfer the mixture to the fondue pot, place it over a candle or burner to keep warm, and serve with crusty bread cubes for dipping.

**Fritters (Jamaica)**

**Ingredients:**

- 1 1/2 cups all-purpose flour
- 1 teaspoon baking powder
- 1/2 teaspoon salt
- 1/2 teaspoon ground allspice
- 1/4 teaspoon ground cinnamon
- 1/2 cup grated coconut (optional)
- 1/2 cup water (or more for desired consistency)
- 1/4 cup sugar (optional)
- Oil for frying

**Instructions:**

1. In a large bowl, combine the flour, baking powder, salt, allspice, cinnamon, and grated coconut.
2. Gradually add the water, mixing until you get a thick batter. If you like your fritters slightly sweet, add sugar to the batter.
3. Heat oil in a deep frying pan over medium heat.
4. Drop spoonfuls of batter into the hot oil and fry until golden brown, about 3-4 minutes on each side.
5. Drain on paper towels and serve warm.

## Dolmas (Greece)

**Ingredients:**

- 1 jar grape leaves, drained and rinsed
- 1 cup cooked rice
- 1/2 lb ground lamb or beef
- 1 small onion, finely chopped
- 1/4 cup fresh dill, chopped
- 1/4 cup fresh parsley, chopped
- 1 teaspoon ground cinnamon
- 1/2 teaspoon ground allspice
- Juice of 1 lemon
- 2 tablespoons olive oil
- Salt and pepper to taste

**Instructions:**

1. In a bowl, combine the cooked rice, ground lamb (or beef), onion, dill, parsley, cinnamon, allspice, lemon juice, olive oil, salt, and pepper. Mix well.
2. Lay a grape leaf flat on a surface, with the vein side up. Place a spoonful of filling in the center of the leaf.
3. Fold in the sides of the leaf, then roll up tightly to form a small cigar-shaped parcel.
4. Place the dolmas in a large pot, layering them tightly together. Cover with water and drizzle with a bit of olive oil and lemon juice.
5. Bring to a simmer and cook for about 30-40 minutes, until the grape leaves are tender.
6. Serve warm or at room temperature, with a side of tzatziki.

## Kue Cubir (Indonesia)

**Ingredients:**

- 2 cups rice flour
- 1/4 cup tapioca flour
- 1/2 cup sugar
- 1/4 teaspoon salt
- 1/2 cup coconut milk
- 1/2 cup water
- 2 tablespoons pandan extract (optional for flavor and color)
- Grated coconut for coating

**Instructions:**

1. In a bowl, combine the rice flour, tapioca flour, sugar, and salt.
2. Gradually add the coconut milk and water, stirring to form a smooth batter.
3. If desired, add pandan extract to the batter for color and flavor.
4. Pour the batter into small silicone molds or cupcake tins, filling each about 3/4 full.
5. Steam the mixture over boiling water for about 20-30 minutes, or until firm and cooked through.
6. Let the cakes cool, then remove from the molds and roll them in grated coconut before serving.

## Cornbread (USA)

**Ingredients:**

- 1 cup cornmeal
- 1 cup all-purpose flour
- 1/4 cup sugar
- 1 tablespoon baking powder
- 1/2 teaspoon salt
- 1 cup milk
- 2 eggs
- 1/4 cup unsalted butter, melted
- 1/4 cup vegetable oil

**Instructions:**

1. Preheat the oven to 425°F (220°C). Grease a 9x9-inch baking dish or a cast-iron skillet.
2. In a large bowl, combine cornmeal, flour, sugar, baking powder, and salt.
3. In a separate bowl, whisk together milk, eggs, melted butter, and vegetable oil.
4. Pour the wet ingredients into the dry ingredients and stir until just combined.
5. Pour the batter into the prepared pan and bake for 20-25 minutes, until golden brown and a toothpick inserted into the center comes out clean.
6. Let cool slightly before slicing and serving.

**Chana Chaat (India)**

**Ingredients:**

- 2 cups cooked chickpeas (or canned chickpeas, drained and rinsed)
- 1 small red onion, chopped
- 1 tomato, chopped
- 1 cucumber, diced
- 1 tablespoon fresh cilantro, chopped
- 1 teaspoon chaat masala
- 1/2 teaspoon cumin powder
- 1/2 teaspoon red chili powder
- Juice of 1 lemon
- Salt to taste

**Instructions:**

1. In a bowl, combine the chickpeas, red onion, tomato, cucumber, and cilantro.
2. Sprinkle with chaat masala, cumin powder, red chili powder, and salt. Stir to combine.
3. Drizzle with lemon juice and toss again.
4. Serve chilled or at room temperature as a light appetizer or snack.

## Tacos (Mexico)

**Ingredients:**

- 12 small corn or flour tortillas
- 1 lb ground beef, chicken, or pork
- 1 tablespoon taco seasoning
- 1/2 cup chopped onions
- 1 cup shredded lettuce
- 1 cup chopped tomatoes
- 1 cup shredded cheese
- 1/2 cup sour cream
- 1/4 cup salsa
- Lime wedges

**Instructions:**

1. Cook the ground meat in a skillet over medium heat until browned. Drain excess fat, then stir in taco seasoning and a splash of water. Simmer for 5 minutes.
2. Warm the tortillas in a dry skillet or microwave.
3. Assemble the tacos by placing a spoonful of the seasoned meat on each tortilla.
4. Top with chopped onions, shredded lettuce, tomatoes, cheese, sour cream, and salsa.
5. Serve with lime wedges for squeezing.

## Pão de Queijo (Brazil)

**Ingredients:**

- 2 cups tapioca flour (also called cassava flour)
- 1 1/2 cups grated Parmesan cheese
- 1 cup grated mozzarella cheese
- 1/2 cup milk
- 1/2 cup water
- 1/4 cup butter
- 1 teaspoon salt
- 1/2 teaspoon garlic powder (optional)
- 2 large eggs

**Instructions:**

1. Preheat the oven to 375°F (190°C). Grease a mini muffin tin or line with paper liners.
2. In a saucepan, heat the milk, water, butter, and salt over medium heat until the butter melts.
3. In a large bowl, combine the tapioca flour, Parmesan, mozzarella, and garlic powder (if using).
4. Gradually add the warm milk mixture to the flour and cheese mixture, stirring to combine.
5. Let the dough cool slightly before adding the eggs one at a time, stirring until smooth.
6. Spoon the dough into the prepared muffin tin, filling each cup about 3/4 full.
7. Bake for 15-20 minutes, or until the cheese puffs are golden and set.
8. Serve warm for a delicious Brazilian snack.

**Blini with Caviar (Russia)**

**Ingredients:**

- 1 cup all-purpose flour
- 1 teaspoon sugar
- 1/2 teaspoon salt
- 1/2 teaspoon baking powder
- 1/2 cup milk
- 2 eggs, separated
- 2 tablespoons melted butter
- 1/4 cup sour cream (for serving)
- 2 tablespoons chives, chopped (for garnish)
- 1/4 cup caviar (fish roe, preferably sturgeon or salmon)

**Instructions:**

1. In a bowl, whisk together the flour, sugar, salt, and baking powder.
2. In another bowl, beat the egg yolks and then add the milk and melted butter.
3. Gradually add the wet mixture to the dry ingredients and stir until smooth.
4. In a separate bowl, beat the egg whites until stiff peaks form, then gently fold them into the batter.
5. Heat a nonstick skillet over medium heat and lightly grease it with butter.
6. Spoon small amounts of the batter into the skillet, forming mini pancakes. Cook each blini for 2-3 minutes per side until golden brown.
7. Serve the blini warm with a dollop of sour cream, a spoonful of caviar, and a sprinkle of chives.

## Dim Sum (China)

**Ingredients:**

- 1/2 lb ground pork or shrimp (or a mix of both)
- 1/4 cup chopped water chestnuts (optional)
- 1/4 cup chopped mushrooms (shiitake or button)
- 2 teaspoons soy sauce
- 1 teaspoon sesame oil
- 1/2 teaspoon grated ginger
- 1 tablespoon rice vinegar
- 1 tablespoon cornstarch
- 20-24 dumpling wrappers (store-bought or homemade)

**Instructions:**

1. In a bowl, mix together the ground pork or shrimp, water chestnuts, mushrooms, soy sauce, sesame oil, ginger, rice vinegar, and cornstarch.
2. Place a spoonful of the filling in the center of each dumpling wrapper.
3. Moisten the edges of the wrapper with water, then fold and pleat to seal the dumpling, creating a pouch.
4. Steam the dumplings in a bamboo or metal steamer for about 10 minutes, or until the filling is cooked through.
5. Serve the dim sum with soy sauce or chili oil for dipping.

## Croquettes (France)

**Ingredients:**

- 1 cup mashed potatoes (preferably chilled)
- 1/2 cup cooked ham or chicken, finely chopped
- 1/4 cup grated cheese (Gruyère or cheddar)
- 1/4 teaspoon salt
- 1/4 teaspoon pepper
- 1 egg, beaten
- 1/2 cup breadcrumbs
- Oil for frying

**Instructions:**

1. In a bowl, combine the mashed potatoes, ham or chicken, cheese, salt, and pepper.
2. Shape the mixture into small cylinders or balls.
3. Dip each croquette into the beaten egg, then coat in breadcrumbs.
4. Heat oil in a deep frying pan over medium heat.
5. Fry the croquettes for 3-4 minutes, turning occasionally, until golden brown and crispy.
6. Drain on paper towels and serve warm as an appetizer or snack.

## Bruschetta (Italy)

**Ingredients:**

- 1 loaf crusty baguette or Italian bread
- 4 ripe tomatoes, diced
- 1/4 cup fresh basil, chopped
- 2 tablespoons extra virgin olive oil
- 1 clove garlic, minced
- Salt and pepper to taste
- Balsamic vinegar (optional)

**Instructions:**

1. Preheat the oven to 375°F (190°C).
2. Slice the bread into 1-inch thick slices and place on a baking sheet.
3. Toast the bread in the oven for about 5-7 minutes, or until golden and crispy.
4. In a bowl, combine the diced tomatoes, basil, olive oil, garlic, salt, and pepper.
5. Spoon the tomato mixture onto the toasted bread.
6. Drizzle with balsamic vinegar (optional) and serve immediately as an appetizer.

## Cucumber Sandwiches (England)

**Ingredients:**

- 1 cucumber, thinly sliced
- 8 slices white or whole wheat bread, crusts removed
- 4 oz cream cheese, softened
- 2 tablespoons fresh dill, chopped (optional)
- Salt and pepper to taste

**Instructions:**

1. Mix the cream cheese with dill, salt, and pepper in a small bowl.
2. Spread the cream cheese mixture on one side of each slice of bread.
3. Arrange the cucumber slices on top of the cream cheese.
4. Top with another slice of bread, then cut the sandwiches into triangles or fingers.
5. Serve chilled as part of a traditional English tea.

**Tostones (Puerto Rico)**

**Ingredients:**

- 2 green plantains
- Vegetable oil for frying
- Salt to taste

**Instructions:**

1. Peel the plantains and slice them into 1-inch thick rounds.
2. Heat oil in a frying pan over medium heat.
3. Fry the plantain slices for 2-3 minutes per side, until golden but not fully crisp.
4. Remove from the oil and flatten each slice using the back of a spoon or a tostone press.
5. Return the flattened plantains to the oil and fry again for 1-2 minutes until crispy.
6. Drain on paper towels and season with salt. Serve with a dipping sauce or as a side dish.

## Shakshuka (Israel)

**Ingredients:**

- 2 tablespoons olive oil
- 1 onion, chopped
- 1 bell pepper, chopped
- 2 cloves garlic, minced
- 1 can (14 oz) crushed tomatoes
- 1 teaspoon cumin
- 1 teaspoon paprika
- 1/4 teaspoon cayenne pepper (optional)
- 4 eggs
- Fresh cilantro or parsley for garnish
- Salt and pepper to taste

**Instructions:**

1. Heat olive oil in a skillet over medium heat. Add the onion and bell pepper, cooking until softened (about 5-7 minutes).
2. Add garlic and cook for 1 minute until fragrant.
3. Stir in the crushed tomatoes, cumin, paprika, cayenne (if using), salt, and pepper. Simmer for 10 minutes to allow the sauce to thicken.
4. Make small wells in the tomato mixture and crack an egg into each well.
5. Cover the skillet and cook for 5-7 minutes, or until the eggs are set to your liking.
6. Garnish with fresh cilantro or parsley and serve with warm pita or crusty bread.

## Sautéed Edamame (Japan)

**Ingredients:**

- 2 cups frozen edamame (in pods)
- 1 tablespoon olive oil or sesame oil
- 1 clove garlic, minced
- 1 tablespoon soy sauce
- 1 teaspoon sesame seeds (optional)
- Salt to taste

**Instructions:**

1. Boil the edamame in salted water according to package instructions (usually 5-7 minutes), then drain.
2. Heat the oil in a pan over medium heat. Add the garlic and sauté for 1 minute until fragrant.
3. Add the boiled edamame to the pan and sauté for 3-4 minutes, stirring occasionally.
4. Drizzle with soy sauce and sprinkle with sesame seeds (if using).
5. Serve warm as a snack or appetizer.

## Prawn Toast (China)

**Ingredients:**

- 1/2 lb cooked shrimp, peeled and deveined
- 1/4 cup mayonnaise
- 1 tablespoon soy sauce
- 1/2 teaspoon sesame oil
- 4 slices white bread, crusts removed
- 1/4 cup sesame seeds
- Vegetable oil for frying

**Instructions:**

1. In a food processor, combine the shrimp, mayonnaise, soy sauce, and sesame oil. Process until smooth.
2. Spread the shrimp mixture evenly on each slice of bread.
3. Press the sesame seeds into the shrimp mixture, covering the toast.
4. Heat oil in a frying pan over medium heat. Fry the prawn toast for 2-3 minutes on each side, until golden brown.
5. Drain on paper towels and serve hot.

## Pastelitos (Cuba)

**Ingredients:**

- 1 package puff pastry, thawed
- 1 cup guava paste, sliced
- 1/2 cup cream cheese, softened
- 1 egg (for egg wash)
- 1 tablespoon sugar (optional)

**Instructions:**

1. Preheat the oven to 375°F (190°C). Line a baking sheet with parchment paper.
2. Roll out the puff pastry and cut into squares (about 3 inches on each side).
3. In the center of each square, place a slice of guava paste and a small spoonful of cream cheese.
4. Fold the pastry over the filling to form a triangle or rectangle and press the edges to seal.
5. Brush the tops of the pastelitos with a beaten egg and sprinkle with sugar (if desired).
6. Bake for 15-20 minutes or until golden brown and puffed.
7. Let cool slightly before serving.

# Borscht with Sour Cream (Ukraine)

## Ingredients:

- 2 medium beets, peeled and grated
- 1 onion, chopped
- 1 carrot, chopped
- 1 potato, peeled and diced
- 4 cups vegetable or beef broth
- 1 tablespoon vegetable oil
- 1 tablespoon vinegar
- 1 tablespoon sugar
- 1/2 head of cabbage, shredded
- 2 cloves garlic, minced
- 1 bay leaf
- Salt and pepper to taste
- Sour cream (for serving)
- Fresh dill (for garnish)

## Instructions:

1. Heat oil in a large pot over medium heat. Add the onion and carrot and cook until softened (about 5-7 minutes).
2. Add the grated beets, potato, cabbage, and garlic, and stir to combine.
3. Pour in the broth, vinegar, sugar, and bay leaf. Bring to a boil, then reduce heat and simmer for about 30-40 minutes, until the vegetables are tender.
4. Season with salt and pepper to taste.
5. Serve hot, topped with a dollop of sour cream and garnished with fresh dill.

## Arepas (Colombia)

**Ingredients:**

- 2 cups arepa flour (precooked cornmeal)
- 1 1/2 cups warm water
- 1 teaspoon salt
- 1 tablespoon butter (optional)

**Instructions:**

1. In a bowl, mix the arepa flour, salt, and warm water. Stir until the dough forms and is smooth.
2. Let the dough rest for about 5 minutes, then divide it into small balls.
3. Flatten each ball into a disc about 1/2 inch thick.
4. Heat a griddle or skillet over medium heat and cook the arepas for about 5-7 minutes on each side, until golden brown and crispy.
5. If desired, split the arepas and fill with cheese, meats, or other toppings. Serve warm.

## Roti Canai (Malaysia)

**Ingredients:**

- 2 cups all-purpose flour
- 1 teaspoon salt
- 1 tablespoon sugar
- 1/2 cup water (more if needed)
- 1/4 cup ghee or vegetable oil

**Instructions:**

1. In a bowl, combine the flour, salt, and sugar.
2. Gradually add the water, stirring to form a dough. Knead for about 10 minutes, until smooth and elastic.
3. Divide the dough into small balls (about 8-10). Coat each ball with a little oil, cover, and let rest for at least 30 minutes.
4. On a greased surface, flatten each dough ball into a thin, round disc.
5. Heat a pan or griddle over medium-high heat. Cook each roti for 2-3 minutes on each side, until golden and slightly crispy.
6. Serve with curry or dhal.

## Meat Pie (Australia)

**Ingredients:**

- 1 lb ground beef
- 1 onion, chopped
- 1 carrot, grated
- 1/2 cup beef broth
- 1 tablespoon Worcestershire sauce
- 2 teaspoons tomato paste
- 2 tablespoons flour
- Salt and pepper to taste
- 2 sheets puff pastry
- 1 egg (for egg wash)

**Instructions:**

1. Preheat the oven to 400°F (200°C).
2. In a skillet, cook the ground beef and onion over medium heat until browned. Drain any excess fat.
3. Add the grated carrot, beef broth, Worcestershire sauce, tomato paste, and flour. Stir to combine and cook for 5-7 minutes until the mixture thickens.
4. Roll out the puff pastry and cut into circles to fit your pie tins. Fill each pastry base with the meat mixture.
5. Place a second pastry circle on top, sealing the edges. Brush the top with a beaten egg.
6. Bake for 20-25 minutes, or until the pies are golden brown and puffed.

## Sarmale (Romania)

**Ingredients:**

- 1 lb ground pork or beef
- 1/2 cup rice
- 1 onion, chopped
- 1 tablespoon paprika
- 1/2 teaspoon thyme
- 1/4 teaspoon black pepper
- 1 large sauerkraut, drained and chopped (or use fresh cabbage leaves, blanched)
- 1/4 cup tomato paste
- 2 cups water or broth

**Instructions:**

1. In a bowl, mix the ground meat, rice, onion, paprika, thyme, and black pepper.
2. Soften the cabbage leaves (if using fresh) or use the sauerkraut leaves.
3. Place a spoonful of the meat mixture in the center of each cabbage leaf and roll tightly.
4. Layer the sarmale in a large pot, covering each layer with tomato paste and some water or broth.
5. Cover the pot, bring to a simmer, and cook for about 1.5 to 2 hours, adding more water if needed.
6. Serve with sour cream and polenta.

# Keftedes (Greece)

## Ingredients:

- 1 lb ground beef or lamb
- 1/2 cup breadcrumbs
- 1/4 cup parsley, chopped
- 1/2 onion, grated
- 1 egg
- 2 cloves garlic, minced
- 1 teaspoon oregano
- Salt and pepper to taste
- Olive oil for frying

## Instructions:

1. In a bowl, combine the ground meat, breadcrumbs, parsley, grated onion, egg, garlic, oregano, salt, and pepper. Mix well.
2. Shape the mixture into small meatballs or patties.
3. Heat olive oil in a skillet over medium heat. Fry the keftedes for about 4-5 minutes per side, until golden brown and cooked through.
4. Serve with tzatziki sauce and a side of pita bread.

## Patatas Bravas (Spain)

### Ingredients:

- 4 large potatoes, peeled and diced
- 1/4 cup olive oil
- Salt and pepper to taste
- 1/2 cup tomato sauce
- 1 teaspoon smoked paprika
- 1/2 teaspoon garlic powder
- 1 tablespoon sherry vinegar

### Instructions:

1. Preheat the oven to 400°F (200°C).
2. Toss the diced potatoes with olive oil, salt, and pepper. Spread them out on a baking sheet.
3. Roast the potatoes for 25-30 minutes, or until crispy and golden brown.
4. Meanwhile, make the sauce: In a saucepan, heat the tomato sauce, smoked paprika, garlic powder, and sherry vinegar. Simmer for 5 minutes.
5. Serve the roasted potatoes topped with the spicy tomato sauce.

# Vareniki (Ukraine)

**Ingredients for Dough:**

- 2 cups all-purpose flour
- 1 egg
- 1/2 cup water
- 1/4 teaspoon salt

**Ingredients for Filling:**

- 2 cups mashed potatoes
- 1/2 cup cooked onions, chopped
- Salt and pepper to taste

**Instructions:**

1. For the dough, mix the flour, egg, water, and salt to form a dough. Knead for about 10 minutes and let it rest for 30 minutes.
2. For the filling, combine the mashed potatoes with the cooked onions, salt, and pepper.
3. Roll out the dough on a floured surface and cut into circles.
4. Place a spoonful of filling in the center of each circle and fold the dough over to seal.
5. Boil the vareniki in salted water for about 5-7 minutes, or until they float to the surface.
6. Serve with sour cream.

## Malasadas (Portugal)

**Ingredients:**

- 1/2 cup warm milk
- 2 teaspoons active dry yeast
- 1/4 cup sugar
- 2 cups all-purpose flour
- 1/4 teaspoon salt
- 2 eggs
- 2 tablespoons butter, melted
- Vegetable oil for frying
- Sugar for dusting

**Instructions:**

1. In a bowl, dissolve the yeast in warm milk with sugar. Let sit for 5 minutes until foamy.
2. In a large bowl, combine the flour, salt, eggs, melted butter, and yeast mixture. Knead the dough until smooth, then let it rise for about 1 hour.
3. Heat oil in a deep fryer or large pot to 350°F (175°C).
4. Shape the dough into small balls and fry for 3-4 minutes until golden brown.
5. Drain on paper towels and dust with sugar before serving.

www.ingramcontent.com/pod-product-compliance
Lightning Source LLC
LaVergne TN
LVHW081339060526
838201LV00055B/2749